LEGACY IN STONE
THE RIDEAU CORRIDOR

FIONA SPALDING-SMITH
BARBARA A. HUMPHREYS

LEGACY IN STONE
THE RIDEAU CORRIDOR

FIONA SPALDING-SMITH
BARBARA A. HUMPHREYS

The BOSTON
MILLS PRESS

03 02 01 00 99   1 2 3 4 5

Design Mary Firth
Printed and bound in Hong Kong by Book Art Inc., Toronto

We acknowledge for their financial support of our publishing program the Government of Canada through the Book Publishing Industry Development Program (BPIDP), the Canada Council, and the Ontario Arts Council.

Published in 1999 by
BOSTON MILLS PRESS
132 Main Street
Erin, Ontario N0B 1T0
Tel 519-833-2407
Fax 519-833-2195
e-mail books@boston-mills.on.ca
www.boston-mills.on.ca

An affiliate of
STODDART PUBLISHING CO. LIMITED
34 Lesmill Road
Toronto, Ontario, Canada
M3B 2T6
Tel 416-445-3333
Fax 416-445-5967
e-mail gdsinc@genpub.com

Cataloging in Publication Data
Spalding-Smith, Fiona
    Legacy in stone : the Rideau corridor
Includes bibliographical references.
ISBN 1-55046-213-X
1. Stone buildings - Ontario - Rideau Canal Region.
2. Rideau Canal Region (Ont.) - Description and travel.
I. Humphreys, Barbara A. II. Title.
NA746.O5S67 1999   721'0551'097137   97-932412-2

FRONT JACKET:
The arched opening of the sluiceway and one of the original grindstones of Watson's Mill, Manotick.
BACK JACKET:
Lindsay House, Kars.

PAGES 6–7:
The spectacular Hog's Back Rapids in Ottawa, at the place where the Rideau River and Rideau Canal separate. The name is derived from the likeness of the stone configuration to a hog's back.

Distributed in Canada by
General Distribution Services Limited
325 Humber College Boulevard
Toronto, Canada M9W 7C3
Orders 1-800-387-0141 Ontario & Quebec
Orders 1-800-387-0172 NW Ontario & Other Provinces
e-mail customer.service@ccmailgw.genpub.com
EDI Canadian Telebook S1150391

Distributed in the United States by
General Distribution Services Inc.
85 River Rock Drive, Suite 202
Buffalo, New York 14207-2170
Toll-free 1-800-805-1083
Toll-free fax 1-800-481-6207
e-mail gdsinc@genpub.com
www.genpub.com
PUBNET 6307949

Contents

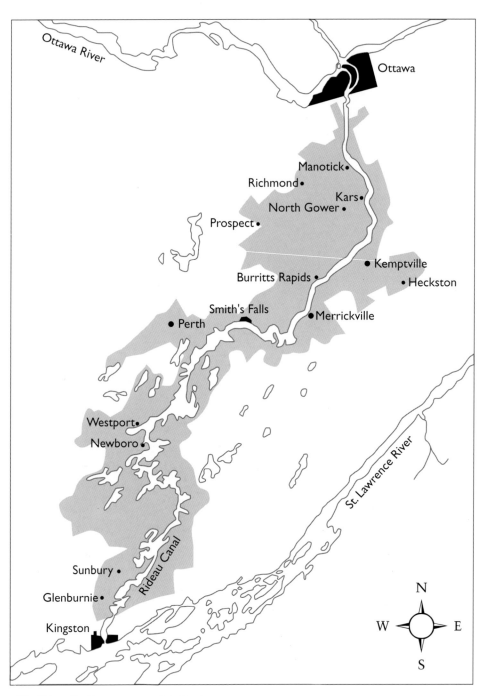

Ottawa River

Ottawa

Manotick

Richmond

Kars

North Gower

Prospect

Kemptville

Heckston

Burritts Rapids

Smith's Falls

Merrickville

Perth

Westport

Newboro

St. Lawrence River

Rideau Canal

Sunbury

Glenburnie

Kingston

N
W E
S

The Rideau Corridor - *map courtesy Parks Canada.*

PREFACE

This book is a tribute to those who, in years long past, created a lasting legacy in stone from the wealth of resources with which the Rideau Corridor is endowed. This legacy, which can be seen in the numerous stone structures that grace a region of great natural beauty, has been protected and preserved over the years by both public and private organizations and a host of individuals.

To illustrate this outstanding legacy, we have chosen examples primarily from the nineteenth century. They demonstrate the incomparable beauty, versatility, endurance and strength of stone as a building material. While not necessarily the oldest or the grandest structures, all reflect the skill, ingenuity and artistry of builders who were obliged to work with primitive equipment in a challenging, dangerous and often unhealthy environment.

It is our hope that this book will make a further contribution to the appreciation of the history and beauty of the region in its reach from Kingston to Ottawa, and inspire further efforts in the protection and preservation of this legacy.

In acknowledging those who assisted in the development and preparation of this book, we would like to recognize with thanks Joan Schwartz for providing the original idea; Ivan Holmes for support in its initial development; George Riley, Terry Smythe, Robert Passfield, Paul Couture, Keith Buck, Chris Papertzian and Myles Gao for information and assistance generously provided.

We would also like to thank the owners of the various properties, who cheerfully allowed us to get just the right shot, and those writers whose works, listed at the back of this book, provided valuable source material on both the history and geology of the area. Finally, thanks are due to our editor, Kathleen Fraser, for invaluable advice and support.

INTRODUCTION

The Rideau Corridor is a rich and diverse area of land stretching between Lake Ontario and the confluence of the Ottawa and Rideau Rivers. It is a region of great beauty, encompassing fields and forests, lakes and rivers, farms, cities, towns and villages, all retaining much of their original charm. Among the finest treasures the Rideau Corridor has to offer is its remarkable legacy in stone. Nature endowed this part of the world over a span of millions of years with a spectacular mosaic of rock. Smooth walls of granite, massive boulders, marvellously coloured bands of gneiss, all can be found here. Man struggled through this rugged wilderness, cutting through the rocky earth to create a canal, one now worthy of World Heritage status. And thanks to the efforts of thousands of labourers, the land inspired a wealth of stone structures that to this day delight with their beauty, truly an outstanding concentration of nineteenth-century vernacular architecture deserving of recognition, pride and protection.

At the heart of the Corridor lies the Rideau Canal. A journey south along its 200-kilometre (125 mile) length commences in Ottawa with a sharp climb through an impressive series of eight stone locks and then moves on through manicured city gardens and green lands to rural fields and pastures. Later it passes between high and tangled forested banks, crosses the shining Rideau Lakes and begins a gentle descent, now cutting through formidable towering rocks to join the Cataraqui River. Jagged, stoney shores then give way to quiet marshlands and its final destination at Kingston, the entrance to Lake Ontario.

Underlying the contrasting landscapes through which the waterway passes is the Canadian Shield, a base of rock shaped by the movement of the Earth's crust dating back hundreds of millions of years.

FACING PAGE:
Metamorphic rock in hues of soft rose and grey add to the beauty of this shoreline scene along the Old Perth Road.

Squeezing, pushing, folding, sliding, with ice sheets advancing and retreating, nature has dictated the location of rivers and lakes, of forest and plain and, through weathering, the character and depth of the overburden.

THE STONE OF THE RIDEAU

The rock formations of the Corridor vary in texture, colour and configuration, from icy blue limestone to tawny red sandstone, from striated pink granite with microscopic surfaces of mica sparkling in the sunshine, to smooth and sombre outcroppings of the ancient Canadian Shield. Huge boulders indiscriminately scattered by retreating glaciers mark the age and nature of the countryside. Roadway rock cuts expose stone in multiple variations of colour and composition. Some lie in flat planes interspersed with vertical fissures, some in wavelike patterned layers, some sharply edged, still

others weathered to a deceptively soft appearance. Limestone, sandstone and, to a lesser degree, granite predominate in the Rideau Corridor, the colour and quality varying with its location.

Limestone is found in abundance throughout the Corridor and can be identified by its layered configuration and pitted or rough surface. Most common in the southern part of the Corridor is the hard, blue-white limestone typical of the buildings of Kingston; a softer grey stone is found in the north. The colour varies depending on the mineral content. Limestone is relatively easy to quarry but hardens on exposure and, while it can be difficult to work, weathers well and continues to be a favourite building stone. Limestone also has another important use in construction: heated and pulverized it produces lime, a key ingredient in mortar and cement.

Sandstone is also widely spread and widely used throughout the region, in colours shading from rusty red to yellows and browns. Unlike limestone, it is not customarily found in a layered formation. It is granular, evenly textured and relatively uniform in colour. As with limestone, the colour depends on the binding agent and the mineral content. Most typical of Rideau sandstone is the rusty red, attributable to the presence of iron. Sandstone has a relatively soft matte surface, which though easy to carve does not weather well or retain detailing as well as limestone.

Granite, most commonly a pink or grey variety, is found in the southern central sections of the region, but despite its stunning appearance its use in the Corridor is more restricted as it is the hardest and most difficult to dress. Smooth and dense in texture, it is basically composed of quartz and feldspar with other minerals such as mica. As a building stone it is weather resistant, very strong, polishes well and retains both polish and colour. Since it is very hard, it is difficult to carve, but while it does not lend itself to use for fine ornamental details, it is widely used for monuments, large carvings and interior trim, floors and stairways.

Marble is seen only in limited quantities, largely in the central areas of the Corridor. It has a limestone base, but the distinguishing streaks and colour variations in marble are related to the impurities and forms of the limestone from which it was derived. It is relatively easy to work with but, being porous in nature, does not weather well. Consequently it is used almost exclusively for interiors, for floors, stairways, fireplace surrounds and trim.

Characteristically durable and versatile, stone has long been regarded as the ultimate in building materials, favoured especially for those structures designed to impress and endure. It can be used in its natural form or cut, carved and polished for wide-ranging usage — from foundations of rough coursed rubble to elegant walls of smooth ashlar, from large and important statues to delicate ornamental detailing. And in the Rideau Corridor, the presence of rock formations so remarkable in age, colour and configuration inspired the creation of many magnificent manmade structures.

Glorious autumn leaves overshadow a solemn grey limestone cut on County Road 11.

THE RIDEAU CANAL

Overcoming the barriers posed by these often formidable rock formations while at the same time making maximum use of this durable building material was one of the challenges facing Colonel By in the construction of the Rideau Canal. The building of the Canal was a remarkable engineering feat, brilliantly conceived, planned and executed by Colonel By and the British Royal Engineers. It was originally planned by the British following the War of 1812, as an alternate route between Montreal and Kingston, to protect against possible American attack from across the St. Lawrence River. Until the early part of the nineteenth century, settlement in the Corridor had been sparse, mostly concentrated south along the shores of the St. Lawrence River. However, with the end of the American War of Independence in 1783 came an influx of Loyalists, and in order to fulfill the demand

for land grants, increased movement toward the north, to the watershed of the Rideau River. Many settlers were lured to the area, inspired by the promise of free land grants, basic tools and implements given with the proviso that the settler remain and improve his land for a minimum of three years. Township sites were surveyed in the 1780s and '90s, and since there were few roads to the interior, most of the earliest ones bordered the Rideau River. Due to the varied water levels and the number of spirited rapids in the course of the river and adjacent streams, potential millsites

Finely bedded limestone sparkles in the sunshine in this striking rock cut beside Highway 15.

were numerous, and by the turn of the century several small mill sites such as Burritt's Rapids (1793) and Merrickville (1796) had been established. While small service areas grew around these and other mills, the lack of transportation limited the attractions of the area for rural development. It was not until the building of the Canal that settlement developed with any enthusiasm.

Work on the Canal began in 1826, and the first stone, reputedly located in the third Ottawa lock, was laid by the noted explorer Sir John Franklin, who had just arrived from the north, travelling by canoe along the Ottawa River. The Canal was completed in just six years despite the difficulties faced by builders obliged to work much of the time in remote and unhealthy areas with the most primitive equipment. While it was conceived and built as a defensible waterway, it was never to be used as such. Rather it became a busy traffic route, encouraging and stimulating settlement in the Corridor.

In constructing the Canal, Colonel By was obliged to plan and develop a route through a series of waterways with innumerable rapids and varying water levels. To do this he devised a system of forty-seven locks and twenty-four dams to overcome a difference in water levels of 84 metres (277 feet) over a distance of 137 kilometres (85 miles) from Ottawa to the peak at Newboro and then a drop of 49 metres (162 feet)

through the remaining distance to Kingston.

The first task Colonel By faced was clearing the land and locating and quarrying suitable stone. While the versatility and supply of the stone seemed endless, early usage was controlled by the proximity of suitable quarries to construction sites and by the availability of stone cutters and dressers. Where possible, canal locks were constructed of stone quarried from the riverbank, but for some, such as the huge dam at Jones Falls, suitable stone had to be hauled from a nearby quarry.

Known quarries of sandstone or limestone used in the construction of the Canal and accessory buildings were located in Ottawa, Hull, in the vicinity of Smiths Falls, at Elgin and along the Cataraqui River. However, little evidence now remains of most of these. Smaller quarries, where only the upper stone layers were suitable or easily accessible, were wide rather than very deep. As a result, most of them and the major quarries also have long since been overgrown and are often impossible to locate.

Methods of quarrying depended on the nature of the stone itself. Thin bedded stone could sometimes be cut using a chisel and maul. Deeper sources, or those with less visible planes, were blasted or split. For blasting, a series of holes, 15 to 20 centimetres (6–8 inches) apart and as deep as 76 centimetres (30 inches), were drilled in the rock, using a hand-held "jumper drill" — a steel bar with chiselled ends. This was a slow and laborious process, the men constantly rotating the drill, chipping and grinding away the stone to achieve the required depth. The debris was removed with a long-handled spoon and the hole packed with "black powder" and a fuse. In splitting the rock, the holes were much shallower and the "plug and feather" method was used. This consisted of driving a pair of metal wedges called feathers into each hole of the series, with a metal plug inserted between each pair of feathers. The plugs were then hammered, the rock splitting along the line of holes. For small jobs in shallow rock, the metal plug and feather method could be replaced the use of by wooden plugs. When wetted down, these plugs swelled, similarly splitting the rock along the predetermined line.

Splitting was preferred to blasting as it was not only cheaper but did not shatter the stone as did the blasting. It was also much less dangerous. Stories of death and injury to workmen due to carelessness or ignorance in using powder are legendary in the history of the construction of the Canal. In some instances, injuries as a result of blasting occurred far from the site. Robert Drummond, the contractor for Kingston Mills, narrowly missed death when a blasting charge sent a rock weighing some 320 kilograms (700 pounds) more than 180 metres (600 feet) crashing through the wall of his house.

Large quarried blocks required for major work, such as in the construction of the locks and dams of the Canal, were removed with the use of hand- or horse-drawn winches and taken to the site by carts pulled by horses or oxen. Depending on the location of the site, this sometimes proved easier in winter, when ice provided a smoother and more accessible pathway than did trails. Smaller stones were removed by wheelbarrow and sometimes dressed at the quarry to minimize haulage and to avoid creating an accumulation of waste on the building site.

The tools required for the dressing of the stone consisted of axes, chisels and hammers of varying shapes and sizes designed to produce a variety of surface patterns. The pickaxe was used for rough dressing; the bush hammer, to produce a surface showing a series of picks or indentations; the point, for a series of grooves in the face of the stone; chisels for the finer edges of the block; and the drove or boaster if the face was to be left as quarried. The pick-faced surface, often with chiselled margins, was the most common finish on dressed stones used in the buildings of the Rideau Corridor.

Quarried stones for the construction of the dams and locks of the Canal and for larger buildings were squared with a smooth-surfaced face (ashlar) and laid with little or no mortar (drywall construction). For smaller, domestic buildings the stone was roughly dressed (rubblestone) and laid in random fashion or in regular courses with a generous use of mortar. The ready availability of limestone enabled the production of lime, which, in turn, resulted in durable mortar mixtures, credited as a major factor in the intact survival of so many early stone structures.

The larger contracts for the masonry of the Canal were awarded to experienced contractors. Among those singled out by Colonel By for special recognition were Robert Drummond, John Redpath and Thomas McKay. Robert Drummond, who built the locks, dams and weirs at Kingston Mills, Brewer's Mills and Davis Mills, was also a ship builder, and it was on his steamer that Colonel By and his party travelled for the ceremonial opening in 1832 of the Canal, enjoying a champagne luncheon en route. Drummond also built the first steamer for regular service on the waterway but unfortunately died from cholera at an early age. John

20

Now well overgrown, this quarry near Elgin supplied much of the stone for the Jones Falls Dam.

Redpath was responsible for one of the largest projects on the Rideau — the dam and locks at Jones Falls. He was from Montreal and on completion of the Jones Falls project returned to that city, where he was active in both public and commercial life, among other things, in 1854 founding Canada's first sugar refinery — a business still in operation. Thomas McKay, a partner of Redpath's, built the notable flight of eight locks at Ottawa. Although originally from Montreal, McKay remained in the Rideau area to carry on a contracting business and subsequently became the founder of New Edinburgh. The handsome stone house he built for himself is now known as Rideau Hall, and is the home of the governor general of Canada.

While Colonel By apparently had little trouble in attracting reliable contractors for the masonry, obtaining masons and labourers for excavating was a different matter. In too many cases those who undertook the contracts for the excavating were inexperienced and had difficulty getting and retaining help. The labourers were obliged to do all the digging by hand and to transport the soil and stone by wheelbarrow to central dumping grounds. It was hard work undertaken in isolated areas. Labourers were required to supply their own wheelbarrows and shovels (a decision taken by Colonel By to avoid the theft he envisioned of tools supplied by the government). There was an ongoing shortage of skilled masons and stonecutters, and advertisements for both ran steadily in local papers such as the *Kingston Gazette*. A letter from Colonel By written in March of 1827 clearly reveals the state of affairs.

I can offer constant work for four years, winter and summer, to stone cutters and miners and that to such as have the means of building a house, 30 feet square, I can give village lots, 66 feet front by 198 feet deep and to keep down the imposition of the neighbouring stores, the workmen may take pork, flour, rum, gunpowder, and tools out of the

King's magazine, by paying the price they cost the government. The miners I divide into small parties, and pay them by the cube yard according to the nature of the work, which is in most parts grey limestone. The masons are paid by the superficial foot, and I conceive there is enough work on the Rideau Canal to employ at least 1,000 miners, and the same number of stone cutters as I have 50 locks to execute in four years.

It is not known just how effective this offer was and figures vary considerably as to how many men — either stonecutters, masons or labourers — actually were engaged on the project. Numbers varied seasonally and from site to site, and estimates range widely from 2,500 to 4,000 men. What is known, however, are the conditions under which the men worked. In addition to the normal difficulties one might expect in working in unknown territories, remote from usual pursuits and living in minimal accommodation, a major problem was the danger to health of working in fly-infested areas and in the swamps of the low-lying areas by the Cataraqui River. Malaria became rampant — a scourge that is witnessed by the many early gravestones in small cemeteries along the Rideau. Despite all the hardships they endured, many of the workers settled in the area with the completion of the Canal, enjoying the expansion of the Corridor that the Canal promoted.

Once the Canal was in operation, the commerce of the area increased steadily. Now it was possible to transport all manner of goods, both domestic and commercial, from Ottawa to Kingston and points in between. Steamships, towed barges and small side-paddlewheel boats carried travellers and settlers with their goods and chattels and animals, as well as the products of the forests, fields and mines. All moved along the busy waterway. Settlement of the interior was also stimulated, with farmlands now accessed by trails leading from the Canal. However, expansion of the area dwindled after about 1880, when railways and improved roads increased ready access to larger centres and bypassed many of the smaller established sites.

It is our good fortune that during the busy years of the Corridor, as might be expected, many hundreds of buildings were erected. Many of these were built of stone — because of its availability and because of the presence of a number of skilled masons who had chosen to remain in the area after their work on the Canal was completed. These structures differed widely in size and style. Apart from such notable buildings as the Parliamentary Library in Ottawa, with its lively Gothic detailing, and Kingston City Hall, an excellent example of fine classical design, there are numerous but equally notable small dwellings distinguished by their fine proportions and beautiful fanlight-transomed doors. Throughout the area can be found tranquil stone churches with modest towers and traditional pointed windows; elegant stone houses, known as stone cottages, in the Old World use of the word "cottage"; simple schoolhouses and civic buildings sometimes enlivened with attractive, fanciful detailing; commercial shops with imposing ground-floor windows, and severely sturdy military structures well-suited for defence.

Each of these structures, from the humblest cottage to the Rideau Canal itself, has a dignity of design and an integrity of construction, and each provides a tangible history of the Corridor. These structures, which have withstood the test of time in the durability of their fabric, speak of not only the technical skills of the settlers but also of their hopes and dreams and their faith in the future, carved out of the very rock of their new homeland — a true legacy in stone.

KINGSTON

THE STONE FRIGATE, POINT FREDERICK, KINGSTON

This handsome building was erected in 1820 at Point Frederick, the site of the British naval dockyards established in 1788 on the east side of the Cataraqui River, across from Kingston. Intended for the storage of naval equipment, with the closing of the dockyard in 1837 it became a dormitory for the naval detachment of the British Fleet and continued as such until 1876. The Stone Frigate became the first building of the Royal Military College of Canada, opened in 1876, and since 1878 it has served as a dormitory for cadets of the College.

Although constructed as a strictly utilitarian building, considerable care was obviously taken in its design. The rubble walls of local limestone are faced with ashlar (the ashlar a 1965 replacement of the original, yellowish ashlar, which had weathered badly).

Well proportioned with a pleasantly low-pitched hip roof, round-headed ground floor windows and a handsomely detailed entranceway, the Stone Frigate is an impressive component of the Point Frederick complex of buildings, declared a National Historic Site in 1973.

The rather curious name given the building dates from its occupancy by sailors, who, in the language of their trade, often referred to their living quarters as ships.

CITY HALL, KINGSTON

Kingston City Hall was erected in 1843–44, at a time when Kingston was enjoying a period of prosperity particularly enlivened by its selection in 1841 as the capital of the newly united provinces of Upper and Lower Canada. Intended to accommodate the expanding civic services and to include a market, it was designed to be of a size and style commensurate with the stature of a capital city. The resulting edifice, planned by architect George Brown, was large and handsome in the neoclassical style — a style much in vogue at the time for important civic buildings — and, indeed, it met the requirements of grandeur.

PRECEDING PAGE:

The Stone Frigate, Point Frederick.

The City Hall, Kingston.

The tall windows of the second floor of Kingston City Hall are set in gracefully recessed and moulded openings.

Recessed panelled trim, classical mouldings and dentils crown each of the end pavillions.

Unfortunately, once the capital was removed to Montreal in 1844, the city of Kingston fell into depressed times. Eventually, and then for many years after, even adequately renting and maintaining the Hall presented serious, ongoing problems. Then in 1865 came a further blow in the form of a disastrous fire that destroyed the market wing. Although rebuilt, the market was reduced in size and the dome and spire that once graced its roofline were then incorporated into the dome of the main block. Further alterations were made necessary when the stone behind the magnificent portico deteriorated so much that it had to be removed. It was replaced with a less-than-imposing wooden pediment.

It took a mid-twentieth century resurgence of interest in the preservation of Canada's architectural heritage and a show of Kingston's civic pride, supported by provincial and federal funding, to finally bring about the restoration of both interior and exterior of the Hall in 1965. The building was reopened in 1967 looking as it did almost a hundred years ago — well constructed of stunning local limestone, beautifully and consistently detailed inside and out, and one of the finest examples of the neoclassical style in Canada.

THE SHOAL TOWER, KINGSTON

The Shoal Tower is one of six Martello towers, dating from 1845, erected to protect Kingston against possible American attack. It is located in the harbour, a short distance from the waterfront, directly opposite the City Hall. Martello towers — so named because of the success of this type of design against the British attack at Cape Mortella in Corsica in 1793–94 — were designed to be self-contained bastions for the protection of coastlines. Used extensively by the British, by the mid-nineteenth century they were rendered obsolete, largely because the attacking forces were by then armed with improved firepower.

The Shoal Tower is two storeys high, with walls of rubble faced with ashlar. It is circular on the outside and ovoid on the interior, the latter due to the variation of the wall thickness — from 4.3 metres (14 feet) on the side exposed to naval attack, to 2.7 metres

The Shoal Tower, Kingston.

(9 feet) on the land side. The ceiling, designed to resist damage by attack, is a masonary annular arch some 0.9 metres (3 feet) thick, supported by a massive central pillar originating at basement level.

The lowest level was divided into storerooms and a brick-lined magazine. The main barracks were on the second floor, which also housed a recessed boiler for heating and cooking in times of siege; access was at this level, with a stairway to the roof, or terreplein.

While the Shoal Tower is basically typical in design of the other Kingston Martello towers, because of its location in the water it was somewhat simpler — lacking, for instance, caponiers, small, one-storey extensions with musket loopholes such as are seen on the Murney Tower, located at the foot of Barrie Street.

That tower was also protected by a rock-faced moat, with a drawbridge providing ready access to the barracks level.

By the time the towers were completed, not only were they dated in terms of military design, but the emergency for which they had been planned was over. Never having seen a day of battle, they continued to serve as barracks in a very limited way. Taken over by the Canadian government when the British left in 1870, by the late 1880s the towers had ceased to be maintained. The Murney Tower was restored by the local historical society in 1925 and serves now as a museum, open during the summer months. Recently the Shoal Tower was also restored but as yet is not open to the public.

JONES FALLS

THE JONES FALLS DAM

The Jones Falls Dam, with a span of 107 metres (350 feet) and rising to a height of some 18 metres (60 feet), was the highest stone arch dam built in North America at the time. Located west of the town of Morton (just north of Kingston on Highway 15), it is an integral part of the system of dams and locks that control water levels on the manmade sections of the Rideau Canal.

In its brilliant design by Colonel By and fine construction by contractor James Redpath, carried out in an isolated and difficult terrain in the midst of a dense forest with only the most primitive of tools and equipment, the Jones Falls Dam was indeed remark-able. Suitable stone was available only from a quarry some 10 kilometres (6 miles) distant and was hauled by oxen to the edge of the river and thence by floating scows and tugboats to the site. Huge stone blocks, taller and wider than the men who lugged them, were hand-hewn at the site and carefully put into place in a vertical position with hand-operated winches. Labourers excavated and removed the earth as required, using only shovels and wheelbarrows. The work was hard, the hours long, and living conditions were most unhealthy. Robert Leggett, in *Rideau Waterway*, records that "swamp fever was especially severe in this construction camp at Jones Falls. . . . Many men died and were buried in a small graveyard set aside near the great dam."

Nevertheless, despite the enormity of the problems, the locks and dam were successfully completed on schedule in 1832, and the quality of the workmanship has been well proven over the years by the minimal maintenance required at this site. The only change made since to the dam was the installation of a penstock to serve a small powerhouse erected in 1946–50 at the lower end of the gorge.

33

FACING PAGE:
The Jones Falls Dam.

NEXT PAGE:
Jones Falls carries the name of the Honourable Charles Jones, original owner of the site, whose small mill and plans for a townsite disappeared with the building of the Rideau Canal.

The Forge at Jones Falls. Small blacksmith's shops such as this, though architecturally undistinguished, were as vital to the building and maintenance of the Canal as they were to the development of early settlements.

THE FORGE, JONES FALLS

Just south of the upper lock at Jones Falls stands the old stone forge. Built in 1843 of uncoursed rubblestone, locally quarried, it is one of the few remaining original service buildings of the Rideau Canal. Due to the isolation of this lockstation and its attendant difficulties of access, a forge was considered a necessity to provide maintenance of the iron works of the lock gates and a variety of ancillary hardware. The Forge has been restored and is now open to the public during the summer months, with a "smithy" demonstrating the production of domestic hardware of early times.

The Defensible Lockmaster's House, Jones Falls. The original design standards for the defensible lockmaster's houses specified that "there be no openings by which the defenders will be exposed to shot, except the small loopholes constructed for their own fire." Not all were built with musket loopholes such as these in the house at Jones Falls.

THE DEFENSIBLE LOCKMASTER'S HOUSE, JONES FALLS

This defensible lockmaster's house, situated on the steep path that leads from the locks to the dam at Jones Falls, is typical in plan of the several defensible lockmaster's houses built along the Canal. They were sited and planned to defend against possible American invasion, but were of course never actually required for this purpose.

Designs were utilitarian, and structures roughly square in shape, with a tin-covered hip roof and some-times with a small, projecting porch. Walls were of uncoursed rubblestone with musket loopholes located at strategic points.

Several of these houses, now privately occupied, have acquired a wood-framed second storey but still retain the musket loopholes, now filled in. The lock-master's house at Jones Falls is one of five that has retained its original shape. It has been rehabilitated by Parks Canada and is open to visitors during the summer.

~ BARNS

Barns with sturdy stone foundations such as these were not commonly seen in this area until after the mid-nineteenth century. The earliest barns were apt be rather crude log structures, designed for storing and threshing grain rather than for protecting cattle. However, as the cattle herds grew and cattle farming replaced grain farming in many areas, two-storey barns became common. These were designed to provide a stable on the ground level with a grain storage and threshing area on the floor above. Where possible the barn might be built into the side of a hill, allowing grade access to both levels, or alternatively, ramped access was provided to the upper floor.

The heavy timber framing required for these barns demanded a very firm foundation; this was provided by sturdy stone walls, commonly of roughly cut local stone and could be of drywall or mortared construction. Unless the required stone had to be hauled some distance to the site, such durable foundation walls were economical to build, required no finish and, if

ABOVE:
The extended roof ridge of this barn at Battersea once accommodated a pulley to raise the hay from the hay wagons to the upper level.

FACING PAGE:
Carefully coursed limestone rubble provides the foundation walls for this barn with vertical wood siding, located at Glenburnie.

carefully laid, little or no maintenance. Unhappily, many of these barns have fallen into ruins, leaving only stone foundations as a record of their pioneer past.

A roadside fence capped with vertically placed stones protects Gilnockie, one of the handsomest stone houses of the Merrickville area.

✑ STONE FENCES

Early fences in the Rideau Corridor, intended to define boundaries and provide protection against predators — or the neighbour's cattle — were often simply the product of land clearing, and made up of piles of brush, stumps or stones. Most common were rail fences, composed of logs with an interlocking joint, requiring no nails, no foundation and no post holes — the last almost impossible where stony ground could not support them and drilling through rock would be required.

Stone fences also required no foundation. If carefully built, they were destined to a long survival with a minimum of maintenance. Often more wall than fence, they were 0.6 to 1.2 metres (2–4 feet) thick, made of uncoursed rubble, laid without mortar and sometimes capped with a row of closely spaced stones arranged in a vertical fashion. However, moving the stones to suitable areas and laying them up could be a more highly skilled and time-consuming task than erecting the rail fence, and consequently, even in those areas of the Corridor where stone was readily available, stone fences such as these are comparatively rare. Simple piles of stone were used in some instances to anchor the corner posts of a wire-and-post fence erected in shallow soil. This did not always prove very

satisfactory, as over time the stones would shift, leaving the posts to lean at a perilous angle, providing little security.

Given the inaccuracy of many of the original surveys and the type of farmland, which was in places highly irregular, with heavily wooded or rough, rocky

ground, streams and ditches, there is little wonder that erecting and maintaining fences constituted an ongoing problem for settlers and township officials. Disputes were endless, and from 1834 on, "fence viewers," whose role was to resolve such disputes, were appointed. Their word was law. While the position of

A fine example of an unusually wide and solid stone fence.

fence viewer is maintained by townships to the present day, their purpose is that of arbiter rather than lawmaker.

~ STONE COTTAGES

The stone "cottages" for which the Rideau Corridor is justifiably famous are distinguished by their handsome proportions and fine craftsmanship. While little is known of the masons who constructed the rubblestone walls with their dressed cornerstones, it is reasonable to assume that many of the cottages were built by the same men who worked on the Canal. Simply designed, they are reminiscent of the stone cottages of the British countryside but rather more gentle in appearance.

Typically, the Rideau cottages are rectangular in shape, sometimes with a wing at the side or rear, one and a half storeys high with a gable roof and a large stone chimney at each end. Most have a simple centre hall plan with the entrance door centrally located on the long side, flanked by one or two windows and, in later designs, surmounted by a small gable with a decorative window. Well-designed classical mouldings trim the eaves and terminate on the adjacent wall — these "returned eaves" being a hallmark of the designs.

The skilled work of the carpenters and joiners is also evident in the detailing of the entrance door, which is the dominating decorative feature of these

45

The McCallum house boasts a handsomely detailed doorway with a semi-elliptical fanlight transom, sidelights and graceful tracery.

Distinguished by the fine craftsmanship of its stonework, this house north of Kingston on Highway 15 was the original home of John McCallum, who built it in 1830. Its straight eavesline is a variation on the traditional style of Rideau stone houses.

houses. Early designs, those of the 1820s, incorporate a semi-circular transom over the panelled door; in the next decade sidelights were added and the transom

spread to a semi-elliptical, fanlight design. This graceful opening was filled with wood-traceried glass or, in some instances, fine wooden louvres. Subsequently, as architectural styles changed from the gentle curves of the Adamesque style of the late 1820s and early '30s to the more formal, straight lines of the neoclassical period, the fanlight gave way to a rectangular design, which became the prevalent pattern after about 1835. Although pattern books were available at the time, it would appear that these door designs, at least in the Rideau Corridor, were largely the work of individual joiners, as duplicates are rarely seen.

ABOVE:

Goldrush House, near Perth. It was built in 1849 by Thomas McKinley, a gold prospector whose success at his trade is as evident in this attractive house as it is in its name. While the house is typical in its basic design, the elaborate gingerbread trim adds a touch of the later Gothic Revival style, a style noted for its decorative detail that became popular in Canada in the early 1860s.

FACING PAGE:

The gingerbread of the verandah treillage at Goldrush House is unusually delicate in design and very finely crafted.

PRECEDING PAGE:

Lindsay House, Kars. Typical in design, this attractive stone house is distinguished by its full-length verandah with treillage displaying a thistle motif, suggesting the origin of the owner, James Lindsay, the son of Scottish immigrants who became a very successful wharfinger in Kars. It was built in 1850, replacing his original log cabin, and is still occupied by his descendants.

Strathmere, near North Gower, was built by John Phelan, who emigrated from Ireland in 1840 and by 1846 had accumulated land holdings of 400 acres. In 1860 he began construction of this house of rubblestone, which, he planned, "would be the finest in the township." In it he raised fifteen children. The house remained in the Phelan family until 1955. It is now a conference and seminar centre.

Bold trim of ashlar dominates the design of this elegant window at Strathmere.

CLOCKWISE FROM BOTTOM LEFT:

Skilled workmanship in stone is evident in the setting of this graceful oval window.

Gable doors such as this one on a house in Merrickville were probably originally intended to open onto the roof of a front porch — but since porches were apparently not always built, these doors became known as "suicide doors."

The semi-circular gable window of this stone house near Merrickville accents the graceful front-door transom with its finely crafted wooden louvres.

CLOCKWISE FROM TOP LEFT:

The very decorative ogee window in the front gable of this house contrasts with round-headed designs more typical of the Rideau area.

The rectangular transom of this handsome door on a house near Burritt's Rapids is more commonly seen after the late 1830s than the fanlight style. This particular door has the added distinction of being duplicated on the rear of the house, offering a welcome from both river and road.

Narrow doors with a semicircular transom and without sidelights usually predate the wider transomed door with sidelights, which are more typical of designs after the mid-1830s.

SCHOOLS

OXFORD MILLS SCHOOL,
OXFORD MILLS

The siting and design of this small school, located in a parklike setting in the community of Oxford Mills, northeast of Merrickville, well meets the decree of Egerton Ryerson, generally acknowledged as the founder of the school system in English-speaking Canada. Writing in 1857, Ryerson insisted that schools should not only be well planned to provide a healthy atmosphere physically but in addition must be welcoming and attractive.

The Oxford Mills School was built in 1875 to the design of John Steacy, a prominent architect from Belleville, and constructed of sandstone from a nearby quarry. Walls are of uncoursed rubble with rock-faced limestone quoins (cornerstones) and smoothly dressed sills. The picturesque effect provided by this contrast in colour and texture of the stone is further enhanced by the highly decorative bell tower and the gingerbread trim of the eaves.

Accommodating more than sixty pupils, the school remained in use until it closed in 1964. It has served since as a meeting hall and is now the public library for the Oxford Mills area.

56

ABOVE:

Rock-faced limestone quoins contrast pleasantly with the warmly coloured sandstone of the schoolhouse walls.

FACING PAGE:

The red leaves of fall glow brightly against one of the most attractive small schools of the Corridor, Oxford Mills School.

In its unusual design, St. John the Evangelist Church in Oxford Mills is more akin to the Saxon churches of early England than to other churches of the Corridor, which are typically of simpler styles with Gothic detailing. The interior is consistent with the medieval style, boasting a handsome scissors-truss ceiling. The church was built in 1869 of stone from a nearby quarry.

✒ CHURCHES

With five major religious denominations flourishing at the time of settlement of the Rideau Corridor, it is not surprising that a large number of churches were erected. The earliest of these were small rectangular buildings, often distinguished in style from rural schools only by the use of pointed windows. Stone, lending an air of permanency and dignity, was the preferred building material and was used wherever quarries were relatively nearby.

Built at a time when the Gothic Revival style, with its emphasis on verticality and decorative detailing, was in Britain virtually mandatory for church architecture, the churches of the Corridor almost invariably displayed some element of the style, if only in the use of the pointed Gothic window. More elaborate buildings also had a centre or off-centre bell tower — in some instances acquired at a later date — the bell itself often being a donation from a patron or church in England. Although plain on the exterior, the interior varied considerably — in part depending on the religious denomination of the church and in part on the available local skills.

St. John's Anglican Church in Sunbury, one of the older stone churches in the Corridor, dates from 1852. With its pointed windows, buttresses and castellated Norman tower, it is an interesting stylistic blend of the Gothic Revival style and that of the earlier medieval churches of England. Following deconsecration it became a private residence.

59

St. Augustine's Church at Acton's Corners was one of fifteen churches erected in Oxford Township under the direction of the Reverend John Stannage. While the slender pointed windows are Gothic details common to many other churches in the Corridor, the tall roofline of St. Augustine's gives it a distinctive silhouette. It was built in 1879, largely by volunteer labour.

✑ MEMORIALS

Memorials, whether simple grave-markers placed with loving care or magnificent statues erected in a civic square, were always intended to be permanent. The durability and apparent agelessness of stone rendered it an obvious choice for their construction. Unfortunately not all stone is as durable as it seems and the softer varieties such as some sandstones weathered badly, softening the designs and losing all or part of carefully carved inscriptions. Marble and granite were the preferred materials, but in the early days gravestones were apt to be quarried and inscribed locally.

By the mid-nineteenth century, however, due in part to the increased population and improved financial circumstances of many, marble became the accepted material. Professionally carved by marble cutters, who were usually associated with a marble works, the stones generally displayed a symbolic design and an epitaph, the latter occasionally in the form of a verse. The more popular designs included flowers, clasped hands, crosses, and very often, a weeping willow. Animals, doves, angels and sometimes faces appear on markers of children's graves. While suggestions of the character of the departed could sometimes

61

Near Merrickville, in McGuigan's Cemetery — one of the oldest in the Corridor — stands this memorial to a young girl who drowned in the canal in 1829. The stones on either side commemorate her parents, who died shortly after.

be gleaned from the stone's inscription, evidence of the physical appearance was left to statuary in the form of busts or full-size figures in a pose reminiscent of lifetime achievements.

INGE VA, PERTH

Built in 1823–24 by the Reverend Michael Harris, the first Anglican minister in Perth, Inge Va is an outstanding example of the many stone cottages of the Rideau Corridor. Distinguished by its beautiful door and unusually large, multi-paned windows, it was constructed from local sandstone with mortar from lime carefully cured on site. The only alteration to the original design was the addition of a windowed gable in 1832 by the second owner, T. Radenhurst. The third and last private owner, Winnifred Inderwick, donated the house and its period furnishings to the Ontario Heritage Foundation in 1974 to ensure the preservation of this fine example of Canadiana. The name "Inge Va," Tamil for "come here," now offers an invitation to visitors to view this memorable building and its attractive garden.

ABOVE:

Inge Va at Perth, one of the most gracious stone cottages of the Corridor.

FACING PAGE:

The fanlight transom, sidelights and fine wooden tracery of this splendid doorway at Inge Va are hallmarks common to the early stone cottages of the area.

MATHESON HOUSE, PERTH

This was originally the home of Robert Matheson, half-pay officer, general merchant, and active community supporter. He built it in 1840, on Gore Street in the heart of Perth, together with an adjacent store and warehouse, all backed by a walled garden. Finely crafted of local sandstone with accented tooled quoins, Matheson House displays the sturdy proportions and restrained detailing of the Georgian

An outstanding example of Perth's architectural heritage.

style, softened somewhat by the graceful doorway with its traceried fanlight transom and sidelights.

Both the house and store remained in the family until the mid-twentieth century. The house was saved from demolition by community members who, with local and federal financial assistance, restored it to its present status as the Perth Museum. It was declared a National Historic Site in 1966.

Matheson House is only one of a streetscape of stone buildings on Gore Street, Perth's main avenue, for which the town is distinguished. Many of these commercial buildings were constructed between the 1830s and 1850s, built flush with the street as was the custom of the time. While varying in details, they are consistent in scale and size. A number of these fine structures have been carefully restored but adapted to meet the requirements of present-day living, recreating the nineteenth-century ambience of this handsome and elegant town.

65

Smiths Falls

WOODS MILLS COMPLEX, SMITHS FALLS

This fine mill complex has evolved over the years from two mills, one stone and one wood, erected on this site between 1852 and 1855 by Abel Russell Ward, one of the first permanent settlers of Smiths Falls. The complex was purchased in 1880 by Alexander Wood, who updated the machinery of the stone mill and changed the gabled roof to a mansard design to increase the storage capacity of the attic. In 1890 he replaced the wooden mill with a five-storey limestone mill with a two-storey office wing. This handsome new mill, with its mansard roof, arched window openings and iron cresting, was joined to the older structure by

ABOVE:

The Woods Mills Complex, Smiths Falls. Once an important industrial complex, this building now houses a fine museum devoted to the history of the Rideau Canal.

FACING PAGE:

A shelf-like bed of limestone provides a secure base for the massive stone walls of the Woods Mill.

a grain storage elevator of metal-covered wood constructed on a tall rubblestone foundation.

Both of Wood's mills boasted the latest in milling technology but their success was short lived, and increasing competition from larger mills eventually forced their closure in 1924. For a few years, space in the newer building was rented for offices and apartments but gradually it too fell into disuse, and in 1981 the complex was bought by Parks Canada. Funds from public and private sources made possible the restoration of the exterior of the complex to its 1892 appearance. The interior of the west block and part of the tower were redesigned to accommodate the Rideau Canal offices and the Rideau Canal Museum, which opened in 1991. The museum's models, artifacts, interactive computer displays, and a large diorama present a comprehensive history of the building and development of the Rideau Canal.

Woods Mill, Smiths Falls. The decorative heads of the tie rods and evenly spaced windows create an interesting pattern on this wall of the West Mill.

MERRICKVILLE

MERRICKVILLE BLOCKHOUSE, MERRICKVILLE

The Merrickville Blockhouse, overlooking the locks, was completed in 1832 and was the largest of the four erected by Colonel By at sites considered key points in the defence of the Canal. These very solid structures were designed to house troops and supplies when required and to accommodate the lockmasters as well.

Built to Colonel By's specifications, the blockhouses were two storeys high and square in plan with tin-covered hip roofs. The base, or lower level, was of uncoursed rubblestone 0.9 to 1.2 metres (3–4 feet) thick, and the upper section of tin-covered squared timbers projected some 46 centimetres (18 inches) from the base. Access to these buildings was by way of an exterior stairway to the upper levels. The only openings in the lower levels were ventilation slits of an ingenious design, constructed with an interior baffle of stone. No doubt admirably designed for defence, the blockhouses did not provide the best of living quarters but ironically were never used for defence purposes and served primarily as accommodation for the lockmasters.

The lockmaster in Merrickville occupied the upper floor of this blockhouse until the turn of the century, and occasionally the ground floor was used as a church. Subsequently the building served as a community meeting hall, then as a storage facility, and finally in the 1960s it was restored by the federal government and now houses a popular museum operated by the Merrickville and District Historical Society.

The Merrickville Blockhouse has stood guard
over the Canal for the past 165 years.

THE JAKES BLOCK, MERRICKVILLE

Anchoring the main intersection of Merrickville, the imposing Jakes Block speaks eloquently of the optimism of the town merchants of the 1860s and '70s, the era in which it was built. It was started but, for financial reasons, not completed by a prominent member of the community, E. H. Whitmarsh. The building was acquired in 1871 by Samuel Jakes, a local merchant who had constructed a handsome home on the adjacent property — now the Sam Jakes Inn.

Once the largest store in the area, it stocked a great variety of items such as clothing, dry goods and china, serving the needs of the surrounding community. However, due to a gradual decline in the economy and in the commercial importance of the town, the store gradually fell into disuse and was empty by 1943. It was then converted for office space on the lower floors and living accommodation above. So it served until 1961 when it again became empty. Unused until the late '70s, the building has undergone a second renewal and now houses a number of enterprises including a restaurant, pub, dress shop and antique shop.

Imposing both in size and design, the Jakes Block is constructed of coursed rubble sandstone, handsomely detailed with rock-faced dressed trim on doors and windows and on the piers that mark each shop. The building's other distinguishing features include the curved corner, arched door openings and an elaborate bracketed cornice. The interior boasts a decoratively painted ceiling, now restored to its former glory.

ABOVE:

An elaborately detailed and imposing cornice crowns the Jakes Block.

RIGHT:

In contrast with the broad design of the cornice of the Jakes Block, lighter and more decorative details trim the roofline of the adjacent building, the original home of Mr. Jakes and now the Jakes Inn.

A fine example of the rehabilitation of a
nineteenth-century "department store," the
Jakes Block in Merrickville is once again
serving the public. The Jakes Inn can be seen
in the background.

WATSON'S MILL, MANOTICK

This grist mill, situated in Manotick on the Rideau River a short distance from the Long Island Locks just south of Ottawa, was built in 1860 for Moss Kent Dickinson and his partner, Joseph Currier. Dickinson owned and operated a major riverboat forwarding business on the Rideau Canal and was mayor of Ottawa from 1864 to 1867. Currier was an Ottawa businessman, and his large stone house at 24 Sussex Drive is now the home of the prime minister of Canada.

The mill was constructed by Thomas Langrell, a fine stonemason whose skill is evident in the quality of the stonework here, which has existed with relatively little maintenance for well over one hundred years. The coursed rubble walls are 1.2 metres (4 feet) thick at the base, tapering to about 0.8 metres (2 1/2 feet)

Watson's Mill, Manotick, one of the finest small grist mills in Ontario.

at the top storey; the metal covering of the roof is original, as are the tall casement windows.

The building is basically quite utilitarian in concept, with excellent proportions and little detailing. As one contemporary reporter for the *Ottawa Citizen* wrote at the opening, "It is of a plain but chaste style of architecture — all attempt at ornamentation being apparently studiously avoided." However, he further stated that this was more than amply compensated for by the quality of the stonework, "for we never saw a better specimen of plain masonry than Mr. T. Langrell of this city has raised here on the banks of the Rideau to perpetuate his fame as a master builder." He was equally impressed by the interior of the building, but more by the machinery than by the fine workmanship displayed in the supporting pillars of white oak finished with stylized Ionic capitals, the huge hand-hewn beams of pine, the careful trim of doors and windows, and the plastering of the walls — all details that were hardly typical of small mills of the time.

The mill was formally opened in February 1860, and as described in the *Ottawa Citizen*, the event was

One of the original grindstones used in Watson's Mill, and reputed to have been imported from "a newly discovered quarry in France and of the highest quality." Since the quality of the grindstones determined the quality of the product, well-cut, durable stones were a prime requirement of a good grinding mill. Stones of sandstone and granite, imported from Britain, were commonly used in grist mills for the grinding of feed grains. For flour milling, finer stones, permitting finer cutting, were imported from Europe. Patterns in the stone, designed to provide a shearing surface that would deliver a fine grind, were created by the mason, who picked out furrows in the stone, interlacing them with fine parallel grooves in a variety of designs.

one "which those present will long remember.... Hunger being appeased, liquids supplied the places of vanished solids and then speeches and sentiments, sparkling with wit and humour, went round the board and a happier party it would be hard to imagine than was there assembled within the walls of the Long Island Mill."

Sadly, soon after the opening of the mill, Currier's bride of a few months was killed in a tragic accident in the mill (her ghost is reported to haunt the site to this day) and Currier resigned from the partnership. Dickinson extended his holdings, building wool and carding mills adjacent to the grist mill and a saw and bung mill on the opposite shore. None of these later mills remain. The wool and carding mills were destroyed by fire in 1869, and when the saw and bung mill met the same fate twenty years later, only the bung mill was rebuilt and was operated from the main mill by a steel cable strung across the river.

The mill produced flour and ground grain for cattle feed until the early twentieth century, when production was largely limited to cattle feed. Flour was produced for only a few years in the 1930s. In 1972 the mill was purchased by the Rideau Valley Conservation Authority from Harry Watson. Now restored, it is managed by an organization of local volunteers. A busy tourist attraction, it serves as a working museum, once more producing stone-ground flour.

OTTAWA

THE COMMISSARIAT, OTTAWA

Dating from 1827, the Commissariat is the oldest stone building in Ottawa. Of coursed limestone rubble quarried on site, at the foot of the locks, it was built for the Royal Engineers as a storehouse for the tools and material required in the building of the Rideau Canal and also provided limited living and office accommodation for the workers. It continued to serve in this capacity in ensuing years with various additions to enlarge the storage facilities; carpenters and armourers shops were also added and the living quarters somewhat improved.

In 1880 the building was described as being used largely for the storage of uniforms and a miscellany of necessities for servicemen. By 1900 it also housed the families of the carpenter and the armourer. Apparently this was not always an amicable situation, as the carpenter kept a flock of chickens that fed on newly seeded grass around the locks, leading to serious disputes with the Canal superintendent, who resented this destruction of his effort to beautify the site.

In 1927 the building became strictly a warehouse, this time for the Rideau Canal system, and by 1955 all additions had been removed and the building was leased to the City of Ottawa in trust for the Historical Society of Ottawa. Subsequently, under Parks Canada, the building was restored to its original appearance and is now the Bytown Museum, operated by the Historical Society and commemorating the early years of the city and the Canal.

PRECEDING PAGE:

The Commissariat, overlooking the long flight of locks at Ottawa, was one of the first buildings erected along the Canal. It looks much as it did when it was built, though probably rather more pristine.

The Commissariat, Ottawa. Sturdily proportioned, of coursed limestone rubble, its utilitarian aspect is softened by the arched headings of the door and window openings. The extended roof ridge, originally intended for pulley hoists, and the small front gable also add interest to an otherwise severely plain exterior.

EARNSCLIFFE,
SUSSEX DRIVE, OTTAWA

Aptly named, "earn" being old English for "eagle,"
Earnscliffe occupies a stunning site over-
looking the Ottawa River. It was built in 1857 by John
MacKinnon, son-in-law and business partner of
Thomas McKay, the builder of the eight Ottawa locks.
Following a succession of owners, in 1871 it became
the home of its most notable occupant, Sir John A.
Macdonald, who lived here until his death in 1891.

The building, constructed of locally quarried limestone, is alive with decorative features of the Gothic
Revival style. Its steeply pitched gables, ornamental
bargeboard, clustered chimneys and the label-type
mouldings that crown the windows are all typical
details of this style, popular in Canada in the 1860s.

Purchased in 1930 by the British government,
Earnscliffe is currently the residence of the British
High Commissioner. Because of its historical connec-
tions with Canada's first prime minister, Earnscliffe
was declared a National Historic Site in 1960.

Earnscliffe, high above the Ottawa River.

THE LIBRARY OF PARLIAMENT, OTTAWA

The Library of Parliament, which opened in 1876, is the only surviving part of the original Parliamentary Building that was demolished by fire in 1916. The Parliamentary Building (known as the Centre Block) was one of three administrative buildings erected in Ottawa following the selection of that city by Queen Victoria in 1858 as the capital of the united provinces of Upper and Lower Canada.

To meet the need for prestigious accommodation for the new parliament, a contest was hastily arranged for the design of the parliamentary building and two flanking departmental buildings, all to be erected on Barracks Hill. Thomas Fuller and Chilion Jones won the competition and were duly awarded the contract. The cornerstone was laid by the Prince of Wales on September 1, 1860. Construction proceeded apace and the building was ready for occupancy in 1865, albeit with both the front tower and the library, located at the rear, unfinished.

FACING PAGE:

The Library of Parliament, Ottawa.

The winning design was in the Gothic Revival style, a style popular in Canada in the 1860s that had received further impetus when chosen for the rebuilding of the British Houses of Parliament, which had burned in 1832. Although the main block of the building presented a rather eclectic interpretation of Gothic Revival, the library was a splendidly detailed example of the style.

Its distinctly polygonal form, while suggestive of the chapter houses of the great English cathedrals, was due in large measure to the practical advice submitted by Alpheus Todd, the librarian of the Legislative Assembly, that the library should be circular or polygonal in plan, thus rendering all contents visible from one viewpoint. The stone walls, 13 metres (43 feet) thick at the base, rise to support a lantern dome some 46 metres (151 feet) above floor level, creating a highly decorative silhouette. The design is further enhanced by the use of various kinds of stone — buff-coloured Nepean sandstone with its many variations in depth and shade for the walls, plainer Ohio sandstone for gablets and pinnacles, and red sandstone from Potsdam, New York, for door and window trim.

Alive with multiple peaks and pinnacles, pointed windows, decorative tracery, flying buttresses, spires, iron cresting and multi-coloured stone, the Library of Parliament is undoubtedly the finest example of the Gothic Revival style in the country.

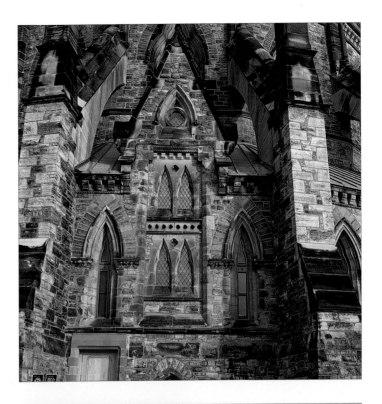

ABOVE:

A view of the delightful architectural intricacy of the design of the Library of Parliament.

BELOW:

Between each pair of flying buttresses is a mosaic of shapes and details in varicoloured stonework.

NEXT PAGE:

Parliament Hill, Ottawa.

SELECTED REFERENCES

Angus, Margaret, *The Old Stones of Kingston*, University of Toronto Press, 1966.

Armstrong-Reynolds, *Ottawa Lock Station Buildings*, Building Report 91–134, Ottawa, Federal Heritage Buildings Review Office, 1991.

Bush, Edward F., *The Builders of the Rideau Canal, 1826–1832*, MRS No. 185, National Historic Parks and Sites Branch, 1976.

Couling, Gordon, *Our Heritage in Stone*, Heritage Cambridge, 1978.

Couture, Paul, *Rideau Canal Construction — Quarries*, Research Notes, Cornwall, Canadian Parks Service, Ontario Region, 1992.

De Jonge, James, *Wood's Mill Complex, Smiths Falls*, Building Report 88-44, Ottawa, Federal Heritage Buildings Review Office, 1988.

Elliot, Bruce S., *The City Beyond: A History of Nepean, Birthplace of Canada's Capital 1792–1990*, Corporation of the City of Nepean, 1991.

Ennals, Peter, "Nineteenth Century Barns in Southern Ontario," published in *The Canadian Geographer*, XIV, 3, 1972.

Geology and Canada, Booklet adapted from *Prospecting in Canada*, 4th ed. by A. H. Lang, 1970, Ottawa, Geological Survey of Canada, 1994.

Hanks, Carol, *Early Ontario Gravestones*, Montreal, McGraw-Hill Ryerson Ltd., 1974.

Hirsch, R. Forbes, *The Commissariat: Survivor of the Bytown Era*, The Historical Society of Ottawa, 1982.

Humphreys, Barbara A., *The Architectural Heritage of the Rideau Corridor*, published in *Canadian Historic Sites: Occasional Papers in Archaeology and History*, No. 10, Ottawa, Parks Canada, 1974.

Johnson, Dana, *Going to School in Rural Ontario*, Research Bulletin No. 212, Parks Canada 1983.

Kalman, Harold, *A History of Canadian Architecture*, Vols. 1 & 2, Don Mills, Oxford University Press, 1994.

Klamkin, Charles, *Barns, Their History, Preservation, and Restoration*, New York, Hawthorn Books, Inc., 1973.

Legget, Robert F., *Rideau Waterway*, (1955) 2nd Edition, University of Toronto Press, 1986.

95

Lockwood, Glenn J., *Montague: A Social History of an Irish Ontario Township 1783–1980*, Corporation of the Township of Montague, 1980.

———. *Smiths Falls: A Social History of the Men and Women in a Rideau Canal Community, 1794–1994*, The Corporation of the Town of Smiths Falls, 1994.

London, Mark and Dinu Bumbaru, *Traditional Masonry Technical Guide No. 3*, Montreal, Heritage Montreal, 1986.

Maitland, Leslie, *Neoclassical Architecture in Canada*, Studies in Archaeology, Architecture and History, National Historic Parks and Sites Branch, Parks Canada, 1984.

Newans, G. Jean, et al, *All Around the Township: Oxford-on-Rideau 1784–1984*, Oxford Mills, Bicenntenial Booklet, 1984.

Passfield, Robert W., *Building the Rideau Canal: A Pictorial History*, Toronto, Fitzhenry and White-side in Association with Parks Canada, 1982.

Peck, Mary, *War to Winterlude: 150 Years on the Rideau Canal*, Ottawa, Public Archives of Canada, 1982.

Plousos, Suzanne, *Tools of the Trade* (Canal construction tools), Cornwall, Canadian Parks Service, Ontario Region, 1988.

Rideau Valley Conservation Authority: Files and Brochures on the history and restoration of Watson's Mill, Manotick.

Ritchie, T., *Canada Builds 1867–1967*, National Research Council of Canada, University of Toronto Press, 1967.

Saunders, Ivan J., *A History of Martello Towers in the Defence of British North America, 1796–1871*, published in Canadian Historic Sites: Occasional Papers in Archaeology and History, No. 15, Ottawa, Parks Canada, 1980.

Stewart, J. Douglas and Ian E. Wilson, *Heritage Kingston*, Kingston, Queen's University Press, 1973.

Symons, Harry, *Fences*, Toronto, The Ryerson Press, 1974.

Turner, Larry, *Merrickville: Jewel on the Rideau*, Ottawa, Petherwin Heritage, 1995.

———. *Perth: Tradition and Style in Eastern Ontario*, Toronto, Natural Heritage/Natural History Inc., 1992.

Young, Carolyn A., *The Glory of Ottawa, Canada's First Parliament Buildings*, Montreal, McGill-Queen's University Press, 1995.